SHAKESPEARE'S SONNETS

NOTES

:luding
- *Brief Survey of Sixteenth-century Sonnets*
- *Critical Comments on Shakespeare's Sonnets,
  with essays on* The Fair Young Man,
  The Dark Lady, *and* The Rival Poet.
- *Critical Analyses of Individual Sonnets*
- *Questions for Review*
- *Select Bibliography*

nes K. Lowers, Ph.D.
iversity of Hawaii

Editor

Gary Carey, M.A.
University of Colorado

Consulting Editor

James L. Roberts, Ph.D.
Department of English
University of Nebraska

Cliffs Notes, Inc.   Lincoln, Nebraska

CONTENTS

THE SONNET IN THE SIXTEENTH CENTURY: A BRIEF SURVEY

English poetry owes much to the Italian, especially for one of best known lyric forms, which, often modified, has been employed by many of the greatest poets, including William Shakeeare. The reference, of course, is to the sonnet. The greatest Italan sonneteers were Petrarch, Dante, Tasso, Ariosto, Michelangelo, d Vittoria Colonna. It was particularly Petrarch to whom the iglish poets turned. The first requirement of the strict Italian, or trarchan sonnet was that it be limited to fourteen lines organially divided into an octave rhyming *abba abba,* and a sestet in iich several rhyme schemes were permitted. At the end of the ocve there was a *volte,* or turn, so that structurally speaking the first ght lines provided the subject and sufficiently amplified it, and e sestet provided the resolution. Almost from the beginning the iglish poets felt free to modify the strict Italian form, typically by minating the *volte* and varying the rhyme scheme.

It has been correctly said that the love sonnet, in its origin, veloping as it did from the love songs of the Troubadours, was he literary equivalent of that chivalry which led the knight of the iddle Ages to show his devotion to his lady by fighting in field or urnament for her protection and honor." In the hands of Perch's imitators, Italian, French and English, the sonnet became iefly a literary exercise, providing the poet, sometimes a gifted ateur, the opportunity to display his ingenuity in the expression love which was entirely fictitious or directed to an imaginary rson. Certain conventions were usually followed. The male lover the speaker; he is deeply in love with a fair young lady whom he scribes in superlatives. But the lady is as cold as she is chaste and autiful, and the man's love remains unrequited, although he cant choose but to continue in a state of adoration and misery.

SIR THOMAS WYATT AND THE EARL OF SURREY

To Sir Thomas Wyatt (1503-1542) belongs the credit of introcing the Petrarchan love poetry into England. Although much of poetry, including certain sonnets, is notable for its fine energy, was also a persistent imitator of the foreign models. Many of his inets are quite literal translations of the Italian originals. But yatt wrote others in which justice in love is dominant and in

which the male lover is depicted as being in love involuntarily ar
expressing his fervent desire to escape from his bondage. He th
introduced what may be called the anti-Petrarchan theme, whic
later writers were to make use of also. On occasion the speak
adopts anything but the hopelessly adoring pose of the abject P
trarchan lover and asserts a manly independence.

Henry Howard, Earl of Surrey, born in 1517 and beheaded
1547, is the second of the English sonneteers. In both form ar
content he broadened the scope of the sonnet, although most of h
are imitations of the Italian amorous poets and develop the san
characterizations and themes. As to form, it is he who introduced
new structural scheme. Many of his poems are divided into thr
quatrains and a concluding couplet. Sometimes called the Surreys
or English sonnet, the form is best known as Shakespearean, sin
England's premier poet-dramatist adopted it and used it wi
greatest effectiveness. The usual rhyme scheme is *abab cdcd efef g*
The resulting effect is different from that of the Petrarchan sonn
in two ways: the rhyme scheme is more obvious and more easi
followed by the ear; the structure is more directly progressive sin
the rhyme scheme is developed climactically and is terminated wi
an epigrammatic, summarizing couplet. There is one danger, how
ever—one from which Shakespeare did not always escape: occ
sionally the poet has said all that needs to be said at the end of t
third quatrain, and the couplet embodies a redundancy. These v
tues and limitations will be illustrated in the discussion of Shak
speare's sonnets.

To some extent Surrey also broadened the scope of the sonn
as regards themes. Instead of limiting his subject to the celebrati
of love, he developed the theme of friendship, notably in the so
nets to Clere and to Wyatt.

The poems of Wyatt and Surrey circulated in manuscript du
ing their lifetime and were included in *Songs and Sonnets* (155
the first printed collection of English verse, better known as *Totte
Miscellany*, which became a source of inspiration to later poets.

SIR PHILIP SIDNEY

During the quarter of a century following the publication of t
poems by Wyatt and Surrey, the sonnet was ignored by poets.
1582, it is true, Thomas Watson published his *Hekatompathia,
Passionate Century of Love*, a series of quite unoriginal love poe

ritten not as quatorzains but as eighteen-line sonnets. And after is death in 1593, his *Tears of Fancy or Love Disdained*, a short sequence of regular sonnets, appeared. These have the interest of earing the closest relationship to Shakespeare's sonnets of all ose written at the end of the century, although Watson lacked hakespeare's golden touch and originality.

But it was Sir Philip Sidney (1554-1586) who must be credited ith starting the great vogue of sonnet writing in which so many oets participated during the last decade of the century. Years bere its publication in 1590, his sonnet sequence, *Astrophel and tella*, circulated in manuscript. It may be argued that without ese poems Shakespeare's sonnets would not have been written. dney's poems (which include some lyric pieces or songs in various easures) are unified in that, following the now established tradion, the speaker expresses some phase of his feeling in relation to is mistress. Sidney borrowed freely from the French Petrarchans, onsard and Desportes, recording a passion first thwarted and en suppressed. Although not infrequently the poet achieved comlete originality and first-rate poetry, he usually introduced the onventional conceits in lines admittedly of lyric beauty. To quote eccombe and Allen *(The Age of Shakespeare,* London, 1903, p. 13):

> Love lurks in dark bush, which is Stella's eyes, and from thence shoots the poor poet unawares: he calls his friends to fly the dangerous spot. Venus, angry with Cupid for not having sufficiently stimulated Mars, breaks his bow and arrows; but grandam nature takes pity on the crying boy and makes him two nice bows out of Stella's eyebrows, and finds any number of arrows for him in her eyes.

e shall see that Shakespeare was to improve immeasurably on is sort of poetry.

DANIEL, DRAYTON, AND OTHERS

Many of the most important poets, as well as minor ones, folwed the fashion during the years 1591-1597, publishing sonnet ses constructed more or less closely on the model of *Astrophel and ella*. In points of style, the sonnet books of Samuel Daniel, Henry onstable, Thomas Lodge, Barnaby Barnes, Michael Drayton, and dmund Spenser have close affinities, and each book bears a title:

Lodge called his sequence *Phillis;* Spenser used the Italian *Amoretti* for his. All are made up of a series of short poems ostensibly concerned with some fair lady, although none is intended to tell a story despite the inclusion of some narrative elements. Spenser's comes closest to sustained narrative in that it does record the progress of his courtship with Elizabeth Boyle, the woman he married. Usually the lady, be she Lodge's Phillis or Daniels' Delia, is no more than a name, if not an absolute fiction. We shall see that several of the sonnets in Shakespeare's sequence, which bears no title, are very close to those of his contemporaries in theme and style. But others lack the richness and the range of subjects found in Shakespeare's sonnets.

SHAKESPEARE'S SONNETS

DATE OF COMPOSITION

Early and late attempts have been made to determine when Shakespeare's untitled sequence of 154 sonnets were written. The chief external evidence is found in Francis Meres' *Palladis Tamia* (1598), a little thesaurus of contemporary wits in which Shakespeare is placed at the head of the dramatists and high among the non-dramatic poets. Meres made reference to Shakespeare's "sugred sonnets" which circulated among his friends. This clearly indicates that at least some of the poems had become well known. In support of this conclusion, it may be added that Sonnets 138 and 144 were printed in *The Passionate Pilgrim,* which was published in 1599. And, since Shakespeare himself called his *Venus and Adonis* the "first heir" of his invention, one may argue that the sonnets were written after 1592-1593, the accepted date of composition of the narrative poem. The line "Lilies that fester smell far worse than weeds" appears in Sonnet 94 and in the play *Edward III* to which the date 1594 has been assigned. But it is a matter of dispute whether the sonnet quoted the play, or the play the sonnet.

The sonnets appear to extend from 1593 or 1594 until within a few years of their actual publication in 1609. The consensus is that most of them belong to the earlier period when the sonnet vogue was at its height, for Shakespeare usually responded promptly to popular taste, as his plays indicate. Many commentators have stressed the parallels of imagery, theme, and mood found in *Two entlemen of Verona, Love's Labour's Lost, A Midsummer Night's Dream, Richard II,* and *Romeo and Juliet,* plays written between the years 1592 and 1595. *Love's Labour's Lost* especially reveals the poet's keen interest in the sonnet, for it includes seven quatorzains and many significant parallels of thought, imagery, and phraseology. Moreover, in the play Rosaline is the Dark Lady who wins Biron's heart. She is described in terms quite like those found in the second division (127-154) of Shakespeare's poems. Indeed, the relationship between the sonnets and the play is indicated by several thematic resemblances, especially the repeated reference to eyes and the stress upon Rosaline's dark beauty. Consider the following passage from *Love's Labour's Lost:*

> *Biron.* Of all complexions the cull'd sovereignty
>   Do meet, as at a fair, in her
>   fair cheek,
> Where several worthies make one dignity,
>   Where nothing wants that want itself doth seek.
>
> *King.* By heaven, thy love is black as ebony.
>
> *Biron.*   Is ebony like her? O wood divine!
> A wife of such wood were felicity.
>   O who can give an oath? Where is a book
> That I may swear beauty doth beauty lack
>   If that she learn not of her eye to look?
> No face is fair that is not full so black.

> (IV.iii.234-253)

These lines bear comparison with sonnets 127 and 130 in particular. It should be pointed out, however, that in the poems the Dark Lady is a *femme fatale*—almost an evil spirit that has enslaved the male lover.

Although the general opinion is that most of the sonnets should be assigned to the years 1592-1595, there is nothing to prevent the conclusion that the poet added to their number in subsequent years. In mood and language, certainly Sonnets 107 and 152 could very well belong to the *Hamlet* period. And in Sonnet 146 can be heard what Neilson and Thorndyke (*Facts About Shakespeare,* 1913, p. 87) call "a note of emotion more profound than can be heard before the date of *Hamlet.*"

10

Notice should be paid also to the so-called "dating" of Sonn
107. Lines seven and eight read:

Incertainties now crown themselves assur'd
And peace proclaims olives of endless age.

It has been argued that the great public event referred to was eith
the defeat of the Armada in 1588 or (in view of the line "The mo
tal moon hath her eclipse endur'd") to the death of Queen Eliz
beth in 1603. Much depends upon the meaning of the word en
dur'd. If one concludes that the "mortal moon" was Elizabeth, wh
was often addressed as Cynthia, Goddess of the Moon, the wor
must indicate, not that she had died, but that she had triumphant
passed through some crisis. Mr. Peter Quennell, (Shakespear
1963, p. 137) points out that 1596 was the year of the Queen
"grand climacteric," when she had reached the age of sixty-thre
Elizabethans believed that a dangerous crisis occurred in one's lif
time every seven years. And since the number sixty-three is seve
times the portentous number nine, the Queen's loyal subjects ha
reason to be gravely concerned and alarmed. It so happened th
the English won the great victory over the Spaniards at Cadiz
1596, and with Spain suffering such a defeat, the period of nation
crisis seemed to be drawing to a close. Those who so interpret Son
net 107 are convinced that it and most of the other poems belong
the period 1594-1596.

The sonnets are filled with what appears to be allusions
references to persons, events, or specific years or seasons; and thes
have been used by critics in an attempt to date them from the la
1580's to 1609. For example, those who believe that the young ma
addressed in the first 126 sonnets is either the Earl of Southamptc
or the Earl of Pembroke are past masters at unearthing internal ev
dence for dating given sonnets. Since in the first seventeen sonne
the poet urges the youth to marry and beget heirs in order to defe
Time the Destroyer, the Southamptonites are convinced that refe
ence is to their candidate, who, as royal ward, was urged to mar
in the early 1590's, but refused to do so. Similarly, the Pembrokit
believe that all this applies to their candidate, who, in 1595, refuse
to marry the daughter of Sir George Carey, and two years later vi
lently objected to the plans for him to marry Lady Bridget Vere.

Some critics use the Rival Poet sonnets in their attempt to da
the poems. Those who favor Marlowe insist on an early date

ɔmposition since Marlowe died in 1593; those favoring George
ʰhapman, in contrast, argue for the later date. The best that can be
ᴅid is the sonnets could have been written anytime from 1585 to
ϩ09. In all probability 1593-1594 and 1598-1601 were the periods
ʄ most productivity.

THE DEDICATION TO MR. W. H.

Thomas Thorpe (1580-1614), described as "a publishing under-
rapper of piratical habits" who, in the absence of any regular
ɔpyright protection for authors, "hung about scriveners' shops
ᴅd from time to time, collusively, 'picked up' a manuscript in
ʰich he could 'deal'," and brought out the first edition of Shake-
ϩeare's sonnets in 1609. His dedication read as follows:

TO. THE. ONLIE. BEGETTER. OF.
THESE. INSVING. SONNETS.
MR. W. H. ALL. HAPPINESSE.
AND. THAT. ETERNITIE.
PROMISED.
BY.
OUR. EVERY-LIVING. POET
WISHETH.
THE. WELL-WISHING.
ADVENTURER. IN.
SETTING.
FORTH.
T.T.

ᴅd this has led to a series of conjectures as to the identity of Mr.
ᵉ., Master) W. H. Many critics interpret *begetter* to mean the one
ʰo procured the manuscript of the sonnets for Thorpe. But others
ᵉntify him as the Fair Young Man addressed in the first division,
ɔnnets 1 through 126. The question, then, is who was Mr. W. H.?
ᵉrhaps it will be well to dispose of the minor conjectures before
ϩcussing the favorite ones.

In his *Life of William Shakespeare,* 1898, p. 391, Sir Sidney Lee
ᴜlled attention to the fact that an edition of the *Four-Fold Medita-*
ɔns of Father Robert Southwell, the Jesuit martyr, printed in
ᴅ09, was dedicated "to the Right Worshipful Gentleman, Mat-
ᴇw Saunders, Esquire" by one W. H., who wished him "long life,
ᴅ prosperous achievement of his good desire." Lee identified this
ᵎ. H. with William Hall, a printer, who, he argued, was the "onlie

begetter" referred to by Thorpe. Another guess is William Herve (or Harvey), who married the mother of the young Earl of South ampton in 1598. It is argued that if Southampton was the beautif youth then this guess is a reasonable one. Moreover, Harvey was likely person to have access to the original manuscript; and he h. a sound claim to be the "W. H." of Father Southwell's *Meditation* since the Southampton family were staunch Catholics. W. Hall, th printer, published anti-Catholic books.

A third candidate is one William Hughes. Some commentato are sure that there is a pun on his name in Sonnet 20, line 7: " man in hew all *Hews* in his controlling." Oscar Wilde revived a old theory that this W. H. was a boy actor. The difficulty, howeve is that in the rather complete records of the acting companies h name does not appear.

This brings us to the two leading candidates, Henry Wriothe ley, third Earl of Southampton, who must be given first positio and William Herbert, third Earl of Pembroke. The Southampto identification, first made by Nathan Drake *(Shakespeare and H Times,* 1817, II, 62-71) was inevitable in view of Shakespeare dedication of *Venus and Adonis* to him and the circumstances rela ing to efforts to get him to marry which have been discussed in t earlier section. The young earl loved poetry and drama and ma well have sought out Shakespeare and offered himself as the poe patron. So goes the argument. A chief objection to this theor however, is that the youthful aristocrat would not have been a dressed as "Master," nor would Thorpe have reversed the initials his name. Moreover Sonnets 127-154 are not addressed to the Fa Young Man. It has been argued further that the earl, as his po traits testify, did not possess that surpassing beauty attributed the youth addressed in the first long division of the sonnets, ar that Southampton, who was twenty-one in 1594, could not be t "lovely boy" of the poems.

The claim for William Herbert, third Earl of Pembroke, fir was made by James Boaden in 1832 *(Gentlemen's Magazine,* CII, 217 ff.). Boaden was in search of a young man "who, from h youth and station, called for no other topics than the Sonnets a ford; who was beautiful enough that the Poet should wish his *stra ing youth* removed from temptation; great enough to be courted, willing and able to patronize a condition that could not exist wit out it, and who actually became the patron of Shakespeare; o moreover whom as the Sonnets tell us, rival poets were courtin

th all the arts, and more than the *charms* of verse." There is in-
ed much to be said in Pembroke's favor. With his brother Philip,
was dedicatee of the First Folio of Shakespeare's works, pub-
hed in 1623. He was wealthy, notorious for sensuality but averse
marriage, and a bountiful patron of literary men. As to the title
1r.", the Pembrokites argue that the use of it was not improper or
esumptuous, since at that time there was not any grander title of
urtesy. Those who believe that Mary Fitton, one of Queen Eliza-
th's Maids of Honor, was the Dark Lady of Sonnets 127-154 are
rticularly convinced that Pembroke is the right choice, for he had
affair with the lady, who bore him a child out of wedlock. Little
inder that the earl remains a favorite candidate.

These are the essential facts relating to the identity of "Mr. W.
." The evidence is not too much stronger for one candidate than
' another, and the question of identity really remains unsolvable
e that relating to the dating of the sonnets.

ORDER AND ARRANGEMENT

Since the publication of the second edition of the sonnets in
40, there has been much discussion regarding the order and ar-
igement of Shakespeare's poems. John Benson, the publisher, pi-
ed Thorpe's 1609 Quarto and, perhaps in an attempt to conceal
it fact, rearranged the sonnets in so-called "poems" varying from
e to five sonnets in length and supplying a title for each. In the
rds of the late Hyder Rollins *(New Variorum,* 1941, II, 74), Ben-
1 "is largely responsible for the obsession for uprooting and
etting the sonnets in the nineteenth and twentieth centuries that
rmastered many amateur as well as professional scholars." If
e assumes, as most critics do, that Shakespeare did not authorize
Quarto of 1609, then there is no certitude that the Quarto ar-
gement is his. Further, some critics, including Clara Longworth
Chambrun *(The Sonnets of William Shakespeare,* 1938, p. vi) and
D. Gray ("The Arrangement and Date of Shakespeare's Son-
s," *PMLA,* 1915, XXX, 630 f.) insist that it is the modern read-
privilege and even duty to rearrange the order of the sonnets if
h rearrangement will aid his understanding and appreciation of
m.

Malone and Stevens, in their 1780 edition of Shakespeare's
rks, initiated in England the still widely held belief that the first
sonnets were addressed to a man, and that the rest of the

14

poems were addressed to a woman. By and large, this remains wh
may be called the orthodox view. The majority of the critics rema
sufficiently well satisfied with Thorpe's ordering of the first grou
but entertain serious doubts as regards the second, in which th
find no particular logic. George Lyman Kittredge, the disti
guished American Shakespearean, was representative of the d
senters. In his edition of the poet's works (1936), he pointed c
that it is customary to describe Sonnets 1-126 "as a continuous s
ries and to assume that they are all addressed to the same pe
son. . . . This idea takes it for granted that Thorpe's arrangement
Shakespeare's." That, however, is pure assumption, Kittredge cc
tinues, pointing out that, if one compares 108 with 70, he will s
that the theory of a continuous and orderly series is not a sou
one. Sonnet 108 "calls the recipient 'sweet boy', while 70 is a
dressed to some one who has 'pass'd by the ambush of you
days'." Kittredge is prominent among those who insist that Sonn
127-154 do not make an orderly sequence. He further points c
that if the Dark Lady "is to be identified with the stolen mistress
40-42, that is further disproof of the continuity and completeness
the supposed cycle 1-126." He could well have added that 129 a
146, which have a general ethical content, seem out of place in t
second series, 127-154.

Yet there remain many who accept the order in which Thor
printed the sonnets, although conceding that occasionally th
order is disturbed or reversed. Gottlob Regis (Shakespeare-Alm
ack, Berlin, 1836) was the first to identify what he described as
logical, cohesive groups. He was followed two years later in En
land by C. A. Brown (Shakespeare's Autobiographical Poems, Lo
don, 1838). Since Brown's theory has been so widely favore
particularly among those who accept an autobiographical interp
tation of the sonnets, it may be summarized here. For Brown,
sonnets are really six "poems" — five addressed to Shakespear
friend, each ending with an *Envoy*; the sixth addressed to the poe
mistress. Brown's analysis is as follows:

1. To his friend, persuading him to marry, 1-27.
2. To his friend, who has robbed the poet of his mistre
   forgiving him, 27-55.
3. To his friend, complaining of his coldness, and warni
   him of life's decay, 56-77.
4. To his friend, complaining that he prefers another poe

praises, and reproving him for faults that may injure his
character, 78-101.

5. To his friend, excusing himself for having been sometimes silent, and disclaiming the charge of inconstancy,
102-106.

6. To his mistress, chiefly on her infidelity, 127-152. Brown
found no place for Sonnets 145 and 146 in his sixth
"poem." Nor did he believe that Sonnets 153 and 154
belonged to the sequence.

The cautious Sir Edmund K. Chambers (*William Shake-
speare,* 1930, I, 560 f.) remained his skeptical self as regards theories
relating to the order of the sonnets. He wrote: "The unity of the
sonnets is one of atmosphere. The thread of incident is a frail one.
Each sonnet is generally self-contained. A few are linked. On the
other hand, there is occasionally a jar in the continuity, which may
suggest misplacement." He concluded by pointing out that "subjec-
tivity has had full swing" in the revisers of the order of the sonnets
as they appeared in the 1609 Quarto.

It may well be argued that the sonnet sequence is not a way of
telling a story. Nevertheless, many found narrative elements in
Shakespeare's sonnets in the order in which Thorpe printed them.
Gollancz, one of the more distinguished nineteenth century editors
of Shakespeare's works, made the following analysis of the sequence, which, with some modifications, has recommended itself to
many:

A. "The Better Angel": Sonnets 1-126

   1. Love's Adoration: Sonnets 1-26 (26 is an envoy,
   followed by an "Interval").

   2. Love's Trials: Sonnets 27-99 (32, 42, 55, 75, 96, and
   99 are envoys, each followed by an "Interval," the
   one after 99 lasting a year or two).

   3. Love's Triumph: Sonnets 100-126 (126 is the
   envoy).

B. "The Worser Spirit": Sonnets 127-152

C. "Love's Fire": Sonnets 153 and 154

Particularly in Sonnets 1-126 he found a continuous story conducted through various stages to its termination.

In contrast to Gollancz, Mr. G. B. Harrison (*Shakespeare: the Complete Works*, 1952, pp. 1592-1593) finds no continuous story the sonnets, but he does provide a useful grouping illustrating narrative elements:

> Sonnets 1-17: The poet calls upon the Fair Young Man to marry and thus "preserve" his beauty.

> Sonnets 18-128: The poet speaks on various topics and occasions and in several moods. The sense of intimacy increases from sonnet to sonnet, and admiration is changed into love.

> 1. At the beginning the poet is shy and finds it difficult to speak in the presence of his friend. He finds himself able to express himself only in writing (Sonnet 23).

> 2. The poet, separated from the youth by the necessities of travel, keeps him constantly in mind (Sonnet 27).

> 3. The poet is an outcast, but the thought of his love comforts him (Sonnet 29).

> 4. The poet cautions his friend not to honor him publicly if he is to avoid scandal (Sonnet 36).

> 5. The friend steals the poet's mistress, but is forgiven (Sonnets 40-42).

> 6. The poet wears the youth's picture at his breast as he goes on a journey (Sonnets 47-49).

> 7. The poet is advanced in age (Sonnet 73).

> 8. Because others seek the patronage of the youth, especially a poet whose verse bears "proud, full sail," the poet becomes jealous (Sonnets 78-86).

9. The poet rebukes the youth for wantonness (Sonnet 96).

10. Away for a spring and a summer, the poet returns to the Fair Young Man (Sonnets 97-98).

11. The poet congratulates the youth on his release from a "confined doom" (Sonnet 107).

12. The poet again is reconciled with the youth after absence (Sonnet 109).

13. The poet is disgusted with his profession (Sonnets 110-111).

14. The poet offers a defense against the charge of ingratitude (Sonnet 117).

15. The poet expresses his regrets at having given away the "tables" the youth had given to him (Sonnet 126).

The next twenty-six sonnets are addressed to the Dark Lady, who has become an obsession with the poet.

1. She is described as being a skilled player of virginals.

2. She is untrue to him.

3. She is of loose moral character.

4. She is physically unattractive.

5. She is false to her own husband.

6. But the poet cannot help loving her.

The collection ends with two conventional love sonnets on Cupid.

THE QUESTION OF AUTOBIOGRAPHY

Before the first quarter of the nineteenth century, the questi⟨
of autobiography in the sonnets received very little attention. It
true that in 1780, Steevens voiced his disgust with the tone and d⟨
tion in Sonnets 1-126, the large group supposedly addressed to t⟨
Fair Young Man. He and Malone, his fellow editor, did make so⟨
effort to find out who might possibly fit the roles of friends a⟨
rivals. As Mr. G. B. Harrison has pointed out (*op. cit.,* p. 159⟨
most critics have tended to join one of two parties, whose r⟨
spective views have been expressed by William Wordsworth a⟨
Matthew Arnold. Wordsworth wrote as follows:

> Scorn not the Sonnet; Critic, you have frowned,
> Mindless of its just honor; with this key
> Shakespeare unlocked his heart.

But according to Arnold, Shakespeare did no such thing; rather
remained impersonal when he recorded human passions:

> Others abide the question. Thou art free.
> We ask and ask—Thou smilest and art still,
> Out-topping knowledge.

Browning also rejected Wordsworth's view. "Did Shakespeare ⟨
lock his heart?" he asked. "Then so much less the Shakespeare he⟨
In the New Variorum edition of the sonnets (Vol. II, pp. 1⟨
165) Hyder Rollins summed up or quoted verbatim the views ⟨
some 185 critics on the question of autobiographical interpretati⟨
of the poems. Of this number 110 reject the theory that Shal⟨
speare indeed laid bare his heart, as opposed to 66 who are s⟨
that he did so. Only 9 take the middle position, arguing that so⟨
of the sonnets are dramatic or literary exercises, and that others ⟨
distinctly autobiographical.

Sir Sidney Lee was a leader among those who refused to r⟨
autobiography into the sonnets, although he did go so far as ⟨
admit that a very few might possibly be autobiographical. "⟨
tobiographical confessions," he insisted, "were very rarely the st⟨
of which the Elizabethan sonnet was made." He further pointed ⟨
that "adapted or imitated conceits are scattered over the whole⟨
Shakespeare's collection," and that imitation and sincerity ⟨
never go hand in hand. George Saintsbury (*Cambridge History*⟨

ıglish Literature, 1910, V, 259) agreed with Lee, declaring that to
ιempt to find the poet's life story in the poems is to follow a will-
-the-wisp, and that we may never identify the friend, the mistress,
ιd the Rival Poet. One other distinguished scholar may be quoted
support of this position. Writing judiciously as usual, George
ʻman Kittredge (S.A.B., 1936, XI, 172 f.) had this to say:

> Baffled in their attempts to discover the undiscoverable . . .
> inquisitive spirits have retired from their assault upon the
> dramas of Shakespeare, and fallen furiously, in unabashed
> discomfiture, upon the defenceless sonnets.

ttredge points out that a good sonnet necessarily appears to be a
ınfession. "In a word, a sonnet must be either patently artificial,
ιd then it is *bad*—or *good*, and then it sounds like autobiography."
ː concludes by asserting that "nothing can prove them [the son-
ts] autobiographical except the discovery of outside evidence that
ɛy accord with facts of the poet's life; and no such evidence is
rthcoming."

A number of distinguished Shakespearean critics, however, are
 less sure that Shakespeare did reveal himself in the poems. F. J.
ırnivall (ed. *Shakespeare*, 1877, pp. lxiii, lxvi) was an early leader
 this group. "No one," he wrote, "can understand Shakespere
ιo does not hold that his Sonnets are autobiographical, and that
ɛy explain the depths of the soul of the Shakespere who wrote the
ιys." Edward Dowden (ed. *Shakespeare*, 1888, p. 16 f.) rushed to
ırnivall's support, flatly stating that he believed that "Shake-
ɛare's sonnets express his own feeling in his own person." A. C.
adley (*Oxford Lectures*, 1909, pp. 330-332), Sir Walter Raleigh
hakespeare, 1907, pp. 87 f.), and W. M. A. Creizenach (*English
ama*, 1916, p. 92) also believed that the sonnets disclose the
ɛt's most intimate feelings.

Three persons, be they fictitious or not, are either addressed or
erred to in the poems: the Fair Young Man, the Dark Lady, and
ɛ Rival Poet. It is with these three that we are next concerned.

THE FAIR YOUNG MAN

As has been stated above, the Earl of Southampton and the
ɪrl of Pembroke respectively have most often been identified as
ː beautiful youth addressed in Sonnets 1-126. There are many,
wever, who deny that Shakespeare intended more than flattery in

his expression of deep regard for the young man, following a lo[ng] established tradition both in England and abroad. This was t[he] position taken by Sir Sidney Lee, who believed that the Poet sou[ght] no more than to attain and retain the patronage of a young nob[le] man, and who emphasized the fact that so many of the poems [are] thoroughly conventional, embodying purely derivative and tra[di]tional elements. But if all this be true, it is odd that Shakespe[are] should on occasion, as in Sonnets 69, 95, and 96, rebuke his frie[nd] however mildly. As Mr. Peter Quennell has written (*op. cit.,* p. 14[?]) "Either the whole collection is a stupendous literary fraud co[m]posed with the deliberate intention of flattering a vain, attract[ive] youth . . . or the Poet means what he says." More recently Mr. Dover Wilson (*Shakespeare's Sonnets*, 1963, p. 41) expressed [his] conviction on the matter: "One cannot read the Sonnets attentiv[ely] without realizing that the friendship between player and noblem[an] was . . . very real, came indeed to be intimate." It is indeed hard [to] avoid the conclusion that the poems were addressed to a real you[ng] man who is portrayed with all the emphasis of passionate perso[nal] feeling conveyed in the language of romantic adoration.

What does one learn about this youth from the sonnets? Fi[rst] that he is surpassingly beautiful. The word *handsome* will not do [to] describe the young man. The Poet speaks of his "love's fair bro[w]" and describes him as being more lovely than a summer's day. [To] him the youth is his "sovereign" and his "Lord of love." Sonnet [?] tells us that the young man's beauty was of feminine cast. But t[he] Poet does not neglect to speak of the "beauty of his mind" of whi[ch] his physical beauty is a reflection. We learn also that the youth [be]longs to the upper class of society. That should be apparent fr[om] the Poet's imploring him to perpetuate his family line by begetti[ng] an heir—something that would be especially important to tho[se] who bear proud names. The adjective *gracious* used to describe t[he] young man's bearing is most appropriate to a nobleman, and [so] with reference to the noun *presence*, which has aristocratic conno[ta]tions. Sonnet 55 clearly indicates that he is indeed a young aris[to]crat. It may further be noted that, from time to time, the Poet gi[ves] expression to a sense of inferiority in relation to his friend, as [in] Sonnets 36 and 37.

If the youth can be gracious and kind, he is not without [his] faults. Much to the Poet's regret, he is on occasion given to wanto[n]ness, as we learn from Sonnets 35, 40, 42, and 89. He even wins t[he] favors of the Poet's mistress.

And what exactly is the nature of this love of a man of mature
years for a youth of perhaps seventeen or eighteen years of age?
Understandably, to many it has appeared strange or even repellent,
for Shakespeare uses words of affection normally employed by the
male lover addressing his fair lady. To him the youth is his "Rose,"
his "Sweet Boy," and "the world's fresh ornament." The Poet's
emotion, which originally is that of admiration, develops until it becomes adoration. But before one jumps to any conclusion regarding
the propriety of the Poet's attitude toward the Fair Young Man, he
should recall Edmund Malone's remarks to his fellow editor, Steevens, on the subject of Sonnet 20, which Steevens found to be quite
offensive:

> Such addresses to men, however indelicate, were customary
> in our author's time and neither imparted criminality, nor
> were esteemed indecorous. To regulate our judgement of
> Shakespeare's poem by the modes of modern times, is sure
> as unreasonable as to try his plays by the rules of Aristotle.

As a matter of fact Sonnet 20, wherein the youth is described as
having "a woman's face" and is called the Poet's "master mistress"
provides complete refutation of the idea that the first 126 sonnets
celebrate a homosexual love affair. The last six lines read as follows:

> And for a woman wert thou first created,
> Till Nature as she wrought thee fell a-doting,
> And by addition me of thee defeated,
> By adding one thing to my purpose nothing.
> But since she pricked thee out for woman's pleasure,
> Mine be thy love, and thy love's use their treasure.

Not to be ignored also is the fact that, on occasion, the youth becomes the Poet's rival for the affections of the older man's mistress,
and that the affair with the Dark Lady is the chief theme of Sonnets
127-154.

THE DARK LADY

Attempts to identify the Dark Lady, who is prominent especially in Sonnets 127-152, have been quite as numerous as have the
efforts to identify the Fair Young Man. Among the candidates are

Shakespeare's wife, Anne Hathaway; Lady Penelope Rich, th
Stella of Sir Philip Sidney's *Astrophel and Stella*; either Anne o
Jane Davenant, first and second wives of an Oxford innkeepe
Mary Fitton, Maid of Honor to Queen Elizabeth I; and one Lucy
Negro prostitute. The Pembrokites particularly have favored Mar
Fitton, since the Earl of Pembroke had an affair with her, and sl
gave birth to his son. But there survive three portraits of the lad
who turned out to have had gray eyes and a fair complexion.

Since, as Hyder Rollins has pointed out (*Variorum*, Vol. II,
242) the Dark Lady is inextricably bound with the problem of aut
biography, date, arrangement, the identity of the friend, and (son
insist) the Rival Poet, efforts to identify her will no doubt be mult
plied. But perhaps Sir Sidney Lee was correct: she may be no mor
than a conventional literary figure, by means of which Shakespea
carried forward the anti-Petrarchan theme. The Italian sonnetee
began early to mock the traditional attributes of female beauty a
Shakespeare does, notably in Sonnet 130. Woman, who embodi
amor sensuale, was depicted as inferior to man. All Shakespeare
reproaches and curses, all his attempts to justify the lady's mi
deeds by admitting himself to be at fault are commonplace amon
the Petrarchans like Bembo and Tasso. The Dark Lady may well l
an ingeniously constructed counterpoise to the Petrarchan ideal.

Real or fictitious, the Dark Lady is a fascinating creature. SI
fascinates by some nameless spell; she can turn the heart hot ar
cold. Assuming that just one lady is referred to, one first fin
reference to her in Sonnet 40, in which, along with the next tw
sonnets, the Poet laments the fact that his friend has sought out tl
lady, who is tempted by his beauty and "straying youth." The Po
expresses his grief, but forgives the Fair Young Man. She reappea
in Sonnet 127 and thereafter is the dominant figure in the poem
The Poet praises her dark beauty and especially her eyes of "rav
black." In Sonnet 128, we learn that she is an accomplished m
sician. Then immediately we are told that she represents evil; ar
the Poet, in a moment of deep remorse, bewails the fact that I
cannot "shun the heaven that leads men to this hell." The love d
picted here is actually lust; it is wholly physical.

In Sonnet 130, the mood changes. In the wittiest, most satiric
poem in the sequence, Shakespeare achieves high comedy as I
again praises the dark beauty of the lady. Here he is the comple
anti-Petrarchan, poking fun as he does at the dedicated Petrarcha
The fact of the matter is that he is satirizing the Petrarchanism of

ellow poet, Thomas Watson. Practically every line of the Shakespearean sonnet provides amusing satirical comment on the seventh
poem of Watson's *Passionate Century of Love* (1582). On the left are
Watson's lines; on the right, Shakespeare's comment:

Her yellow locks exceed the beaten gold	If hairs be wires, black wires grow on her head.
Her sparkling eyes in heav'n a place deserve	My Mistress' eyes are nothing like the sun
Her words are music all of silver sound	I love to hear her speak, yet well I know That music hath a far more pleasant sound.
On either cheek a rose and lily lie	I have seen roses damasked, red and white, But no such roses see I in her cheeks.
Her breath is sweet perfume, or holy flame	And in some perfume is there more delight Than in the breath that from my mistress reeks.
Her lips more red than any coral stone Her neck more white than aged swans that moan	Coral is far more red than her lips red If snow be white, why then her breasts are dun.

Next the Poet charges the lady with cruelty, but nevertheless
refers to her as "the fairest and most precious jewel" and adds that
"In nothing art thou black save in thy deeds" (Sonnet 131). After
lauding once more her dark beauty, the Poet then speaks of her
"cruel eyes" and revives the charge that she has enslaved the Fair
Young Man as well as himself. As he writes in Sonnet 134, "Thou
hast both him and me." There follow two of the "Will" sonnets in
which occur the erotic pun on the Poet's own name, emphasizing
the lecherous nature of this ardent love affair. In Sonnets 137 and

138, the Poet accuses the lady of falsehood, referring to her "eyes o
falsehood" and her "false-speaking tongue." He concludes Sonne
138 with a line incorporating another erotic pun, once more under
scoring the physical aspect of his love: "Therefore I lie with her
and she with me."

Subsequently, the Poet dwells upon her cruelty again, her
"proud heart." In Sonnet 141 he states that, although he canno
help loving her, he discerns "a thousand errors" in her. He then
speaks of his "sinful loving," the "false bonds of love," and her infi
delity. The Dark Lady appears as his "worser spirit" in contrast to
his "better angel," the Fair Young Man, whom she tempts from hi
side in Sonnet 144. He describes his love as a fever in Sonnet 14'
and identifies Reason as the physician whose ministrations he ig
nores. The Poet concludes vehemently:

> For I have sworn thee fair, and though thee bright,
> Who art as black as hell, as dark as night.

The Poet goes on to denounce the lady for her "foul faults," he
continued cruelty, her cheating. And in Sonnet 151 he again under
scores the fleshly aspect of his love with an erotic pun:

> . . . flesh stays no further reason,
> But, rising at thy name, doth point out thee
> As his triumphant prize.

Finally in Sonnet 152, he charges the Dark Lady with being "twic
foresworn," one who has broken her bed-vows:

> For I have sworn thee fair; more perjured eye,
> To swear against the truth so foul a lie.

It is apparent that love as it is revealed in the sonnets was a storm
one, marked by deep passion and often violent emotion.

THE RIVAL POET

The Rival Poet, referred to in Sonnets 76-86, is the third mys
terious person in Shakespeare's poems. The Poet may refer tacitl
to him also in Sonnets 100-103. Whoever he was, Shakespear
speaks of him as "a worthier pen" (79.6), "a better spirit" (80.2) t
whom he was "inferior far" (80.7), and makes reference to "th

proud full sail of his great verse" (86.1) and to the fact that he had been taught by spirits "to write above a mortal pitch" (86.5 f.). For generations commentators have sought his identity, and many names have been suggested. Recently M. A. L. Rowse, a Southampton-ite who dates the sonnets rather early, revived the nomination of Christopher Marlowe, arguing that the phrase "the proud full sail of his great verse" must surely be applicable to him. Mr. Rowse further argues that "that affable familiar ghost/Which nightly gull him with intelligence [i.e., news or information]" is a reference to Mephistopheles, the devil who for a twenty-four year period served Dr. Faustus, the protagonist in Marlowe's well-known tragedy. In contrast, there are those who claim that Marlowe was the author of many of the sonnets, including the Rival Poet ones, and that the Rival Poet therefore was Shakespeare himself!

There is actually no reason why a single rival should be preferred to plural rival poets, since in Sonnet 85 Shakespeare refers to "others" who wrote admirable verse. But most commentators insist on one person. In addition to Marlowe, Michael Drayton, Samuel Daniel, George Peele, Thomas Nash, Thomas Lodge, Richard Barnfield, Barnaby Rich, Robert Greene, Edmund Spenser, George Chapman, and Ben Johnson have their champions.

Ben Jonson's name was presented rather early by one J. G. R. (Notes and Queries, February 12, 1859, p. 122), but has not been accepted widely. It was argued that Sonnets 78 and 80 especially refer to him, and that the figures of ships ("proudest sail" and "saucy bark") are exactly like those Thomas Fuller later used in describing the wit-combats of Jonson and Shakespeare at the Mermaid in which the two were compared to a Spanish great galleon and an English man-of-war.

William Minto (Characteristics of English Poets from Chaucer to Shirley, 1874, pp. 290-292) was first to suggest Chapman, who has remained a favorite choice for many. Minto argued that Chapman's Shadow of the Night, 1594, goes far to establish his identity with Shakespeare's rival, especially since the purpose of the work is to extol the wonderful power of Night in imparting knowledge to her votaries. F. J. Furnival (Shakespeare, 1877, p. lxv n.) joined Minto, insisting that the first line of Sonnet 86 was an unmistakable reference to the swelling hexameters of Chapman's Englishing of Homer.

One of the unique and far-fetched theories propounded was that Dante was the Rival Poet. This was advanced by an anonymous writer in *Blackwood's Magazine*, 1884-1886. He reasoned as follows. Shakespeare calls his rival "a spirit," thus showing that he was not a living contemporary. Also the "compeers by night" (86.7) are Homer, Virgil, Horace, and others. The "affable familiar ghost" (86.9) is Beatrice.

Old theories will be revived; new ones advanced—tomorrow, tomorrow, and tomorrow. But like the Fair Young Man and the Dark Lady, the identity of the Rival Poet will probably remain a mystery.

DOMINANT THEMES

IMMORTALITY THROUGH OFFSPRING

In the first large division of the Sonnets, Time is the great enemy of youth and beauty. The Poet, like so many of his contemporaries, viewed with pain and sorrow the corrosive effects of Time and sought answers to the question of how it could be defeated and youth and beauty preserved. In Shakespeare's sequence three answers are propounded. The first of these, along with the extolling of the young man's unmatched beauty, is the theme of the first seventeen sonnets. These constitute a group in which the youth is urged to defeat the "bloody tyrant" Time by marrying and begetting an heir, thus achieving a kind of immortality through offspring. Characteristically, Shakespeare develops the theme in three quatrains, wherein he generalizes; then, in the final couplet, he particularizes, addressing the young man directly. His initial argument is that the youth owes it to himself and to the world to conquer "wasteful Time" by continuing his life and beauty through his children.

In the very first sonnet the theme is introduced. It should be noted that the poem includes praise of the youth's beauty and blame for his failure to try to preserve it. In lines 5-8, he is accused of harboring self-love, thus making "a famine where abundance lies" and "waste in niggarding"—that is, in hoarding his beauty. The Poet then implores the young man to "pity the world" and give it its due—the propagation of species. The argument and plea are continued in the second sonnet, wherein Shakespeare finds another metaphor, a martial one, to make his case:

When forty winters shall besiege thy brow,
And dig deep trenches in thy beauty's field,

Thy youth's proud livery, so gazed on now,
Will be a tattered weed [garment] of small
   worth held. . . .

he argument is carried forward in the third sonnet by means of a
etaphor from husbandry:

For where is she so fair whose uneared [untilled] womb
Disdains the tillage of thy husbandry?

                                             (5-6)

he Poet insists that the youth is the image of his mother, and that
 him she "Calls back the lovely April of his prime." The poem
ds with the dire prophecy: "Die single and thine image dies with
ee."

Sonnet 4 provides a kind of explication of all the Poet has been
ying so far. In a series of questions and statements, he drives
me the lesson of the right use of one's endowments. It is clear
at Shakespeare had in mind the Parable of the Talents: the wise
e of God's gifts and Nature's gifts is imperative. Lines 3 and 4
ntain the key idea:

Nature's bequest gives nothing but doth lend,
And being frank she lends to those are free.

eing generous and liberal, Nature lends her gifts to those who pos-
ss these same qualities, not to "niggards," that is, not to misers.
he contrast between the youth's alleged miserliness and Nature's
unificence is repeated in lines 7 and 8, this time in terms of usury:

Profitless usurer, why dost thou use
So great a sum of sums yet canst not live?

he term *use* here means both "invest" and "use up." Similarly, *live*
eans both "make a living" and "endure." The inevitable conclu-
on is that if the youth does not make use of his beauty properly
d unselfishly by seeking to perpetuate it, he is doomed to obliv-
n, since he will die childless.

Sonnets 5 and 6 are a set of closely related poems in which the
dividual's mortal partaking of immortality finds expression in the
otic image of distillation, the use of which does not make for an
trusion of its physical nature.

28

A second set, sonnets 9 and 10, deserves some special attentic
In these poems, the Poet develops the argument that

> beauty's waste hath in the world an end,
> And kept unused, the user so destroys it. . . .
>
> (11-12)

Sonnets 12, 15, and 16 constitute a final set of closely relate
poems. Here especially the Poet inveighs against devouring Tim
making reference to "Time's scythe" and to "this bloody tyra
Time." So the major theme is clearly set forth and developed fro
more than one point of view: the youth owes it to himself and th
world to conquer Time, to continue his life and beauty by fatherir
children.

It may be pointed out that Sonnets 12 and 15, so notable f
their musical quality, thanks largely to the effective use of alliter
tion and attractive vowel runs, are of unusual merit. They are a
most always included in anthologies of lyric poetry. Note th
beauty of the opening lines of Sonnet 12:

> When I do count the clock that tells the time,
> And see brave day sunk in hideous night;
> When I behold the violet past prime,
> And sable curls are silvered o'er with white. . . .

These indeed convey the sense of sorrow, of poignancy, at th
thought that youth and beauty must be cut down by Time's scyth
The contrast of "brave day" (i.e., splendid day) with "hideo
night" is particularly good. And as Mr. Edward Hubler has pointe
out (*The Sense of Shakespeare's Sonnets*, 1952, p. 25): "No sonn
beginning with 'When' is an undistinguished poem." The reason
that the structure of such sonnets, and there are several in the s
quence, is periodic, making for tightness of organization, logic
progression, and avoidance of the tacked-on couplet.

IMMORTALITY THROUGH VERSE

It is not without interest to find that the word *time* is use
seventy-eight times in Sonnets 1-126 and not once in the remainir
sonnets. Of this first large group, nine develop the theme of p

ry's power to conquer Time, which is variously described as
wift-footed" and "devouring," reference also being made to
"ime's fell hand" and to "Time's injurious hand."

Sonnet 18 introduces this new theme, along with those related
the young man's beauty and to his temperate, unspoiled nature.
is sonnet, one of the best known in the sequence, is memorable
r the skillful and varied presentation of subject matter. Initially,
e Poet poses a question—"Shall I compare thee to a summer's
y?"—and then corrects it. The imagery is the very essence of sim-
icity. In the second quatrain, legal terminology is introduced
summer's lease") in rather daring contrast to the commonplace
ages in the first quatrain. The Poet returns to the opening image
lines of comparable simplicity but marked by a fuller tone and
eper feeling. Then follows the concluding couplet:

So long as men can breathe or eyes can see,
So long lives this, and this gives life to thee.

There are many classical and medieval antecedents for such a
f-claim of immortality. They may be found, for example, in
id, *Amores*, I.xv. 41 f.; in Horace, *Odes*, III, 30; in Propertius
ii. 21-24; in Dante, *Inferno*, IV, 97 ff., and elsewhere. It may be
ded this sense of Time's hostility is fundamental, not only to the
nnets, but to the plays of the years 1592-1595. Indeed, the theme
s a commonplace one at this time. Usually, it was associated
th the Platonizing philosophy of the court poets such as Sidney,
with the "otherworld" attitude inherited from the medieval peri-
. In Shakespeare's sonnets it is the first attitude which prevails.
tural fear of the action of Time is not offset by the religious view
his sequence.

In Sonnet 19, the Poet assures the young man that his "love
ll in [his] verse ever live long"; in Sonnet 38, he addresses the
uth, urging him to be the tenth Muse and "let him bring forth/
rnal numbers to outlive long date." Again, in Sonnet 54, he ints that the beauteous and lovely youth will not really fade or per-
because the Poet "distills" his "truth." And so from several
ints of view the theme is presented: in Sonnets 60, 63, 65
herein the young man is described as "Time's best jewel"), 81,
1 100. In that last sonnet, the Poet berates his "forgetful muse":

Give my love fame faster than Time wastes life;
So thou prevent's his scythe and crooked knife.

All in all, this group comprises a most interesting and successful ^
of poems.

IMMORTALITY THROUGH LOVE

The theme of immortality through love is developed implici
and explicitly in several of the first one hundred and twenty-s
poems. Not only is the youth granted immortality through vers
but since the Poet's enduring love is repeatedly stressed, the Po
himself gains a kind of immortality. "O, let me true in love b
truly write," exclaims the Poet (21.9). And in Sonnet 22 he argu
that, so long as he holds the affection of the youth, he can de
Time:

> My glass shall not persuade me I am old,
> So long as youth and thou are of one date. . . .
>
> (1-2)

The same idea is expressed in other words in Sonnet 25:

> The painful warrior famouséd for fight,
> After a thousand victories once foiled,
> Is from the book of honor razéd quite,
> And all the rest forgot for which he toiled.
>   Then happy I that love and am beloved
>   Where I may not remove, nor be removed.
>
> (9-14)

The concept of Time defeated by love also finds expression in So
net 62:

> 'Tis thee, myself, that for myself I praise,
> Painting my age with beauty of thy days.
>
> (13-14)

In Sonnet 100, the Poet asks:

> Give my love fame faster than Time wastes life;
> So thou prevent'st his scythe and crooked knife.
>
> (13-14)

Especially in Sonnet 116, one of the finest in the sequence, ^
theme is presented: Love is not love, the Poet argues:

Which alters when it alteration finds,
Or bends with the remover to remove.

(4-6)

is "an ever-fixéd mark/ That looks on tempests and is never
aken . . ." (5-6). Finally, in Sonnet 123, the Poet insists that Time
ll never be able to boast that he does undergo a change of heart:
will be true despite thy scythe and thee" (14).

THE THEME OF COMPENSATION

In at least three sonnets, often referred to as the "despair" son-
ts, Shakespeare states that the Fair Young Man provides com-
nsation for all the failures and disappointments in his life. The
st is Sonnet 25, in which he writes:

Let those who are in favor with their stars
Of public honour and proud titles boast,
Whilst I, who fortune of such triumph bars,
Unlook'd for joy in that I honour most.

(1-4)

e youth's love more than compensates for his adverse fortune.
tter known is Sonnet 29, with its magnificent simile in the third
atrain. This deserves quotation in full:

When in disgrace with Fortune and men's eyes,
I all alone beweep my outcast state,
And trouble deaf heaven with my bootless cries,
And look upon myself and curse my fate,
Wishing me like to one more rich in hope,
Featured like him, like him with friends possessed,
Desiring this man's art, and that man's scope,
With what I most enjoy contented least;
Yet in these thoughts myself almost despising,
Haply I think on thee, and then my state,
Like to the lark at break of day arising
From sullen earth, sings hymns at heaven's gate;
For thy sweet love rememb'red such wealth brings,
That then I scorn to change my state with kings.

In Sonnet 37 there is an even more explicit treatment of this
ne theme: The Poet's awareness of his friend's love more than

makes up for all his own deficiencies. The Poet speaks of himself
one who has been "made lame by fortune's dearest spite" but go
on to say, "I in thy abundance am suffic'd" (11). Again in the bea
tiful Sonnet 30 he repeats that the youth is a priceless compens
tion, not only for many disappointments and unrealized hopes, b
also for the loss of earlier friends:

> But if the while I think on thee, dear friend,
> All losses are restor'd and sorrows end.
>
> (13-14)

This subject of lost friends and loves is the main subject of Sonn
31, which ends with these lines:

> Their images I lov'd I view in thee,
> And thou, all they, has all the all of me.

Finally in Sonnet 66, Shakespeare declares that the youth provid
compensation for his own deficiencies, disappointments, a
losses. Moreover, he compensates for all that "sea of trouble
those "whips and scorns of Time" of which Hamlet speaks in
second soliloquy; and, like Hamlet, the Poet gives expression to
death wish: "for restful death I cry" (1). But in the final couplet
reverses his attitude:

> Tir'd with all these, from these would I be gone,
> Save that, to die, I leave my love alone.

As Mr. J. B. Leishman has stated (*Themes and Variations
Shakespeare's Sonnets*, 1961, p. 209) there is "no real precedent
previous love-poetry either for Shakespeare's topic or for Shak
peare's treatment of it."

LOVE IN ABSENCE

A total of twenty-three sonnets develop the theme of absen
Although none of these may be counted among the poems of
tinction in the sequence, all are interesting for what they glance
and for what they give us of the Poet's mind. Certain ones, nota
36, 49, 57, derive their power from the Poet's fears for the disso
tion of the friendship as a result of the separation. The concept

identity — the idea of one soul in two bodies — was commonplace in Shakespeare's time; and this finds a place in the absence sonnets.

In Sonnet 27, the Poet describes himself as being weary with toil and vainly trying to sleep. He continues his travels mentally:

> Lo, thus, by day my limbs, by night my mind,
> For thee, and for myself, no quiet find
>
> (13-14)

And in the next sonnet he again speaks of himself as one "debarred the benefit of rest," so much does he suffer in absence from his dear friend. In Sonnet 39 he speaks of the youth as being the better part of himself. "O, absence," he continues, "what a torment wouldst thou prove," were it not for thoughts of love.

It is again the sleepless poet who speaks in Sonnet 43:

> All days are nights to see till I see thee,
> And nights bright days when dreams do show thee me.
>
> (13-14)

In the next sonnet he complains against "injurious distance" which has separated him from the young man, but expresses satisfaction in the fact that "nimble thought can jump both sea and land" so that mentally he is united with his friend. Here and in Sonnet 45, the Poet wishes that he were entirely made of the lighter elements, "slight air and purging fire," so that he could actually leap the distance to his friend, as his thoughts and wishes, being incorporeal and therefore free of earth and water, were able to do.

In Sonnet 47, the Poet finds solace in a picture of the young man which he carries with him:

> So, either by thy picture or my love,
> Thyself away are present still with me....
>
> (9-10)

In Sonnet 49 he especially is concerned that the separation may lead to the dissolution of the prized friendship. In Sonnet 50, he complains that his "grief lies onward and [his] joy behind," as he wearily rides farther away from the one he loves. He continues the same subject in Sonnet 51, concluding:

> Since from thee going he [the horse] went willful slow,
> Towards thee I'll run and give him leave to go.
>
> (13-14)

Later, in Sonnet 97, the Poet, aware that it is summer, nevertheless compares the youth's absence, or his own, to a bleak winter:

> What freezings have I felt, what dark days seen,
> What old December's bareness everywhere!
>
> (3-4)

"Summer and his pleasure" wait on the youth, he continues: And, "thou away, the very birds are mute" (12). And so in Sonnet 98, wherein the Poet, with his sure eye for nature, describes the beauties of spring, all of which serve only to remind him of the young man:

> Yet seemed it winter still, and, you away,
> As with your shadow I with these did play.
>
> (13-14)

In Sonnet 99, the nature theme once more prevails:

> More flowers I noted, yet I none could see,
> But sweet or color it had stolen from thee.
>
> (13-14)

Yet again, in Sonnet 113, all things remind him of youth — the birds, flowers, the day, the night:

> Incapable of more, replete with you,
> My most true mind thus maketh mine eye untrue.
>
> (13-14)

THE FAREWELL SONNETS

In addition to the "Absence" sonnets, there is an interesting group, nos. 87-93, in which the Poet says his farewell to the beautiful young man from whom he is to be, for some reason not made clear, permanently separated. In the first he writes:

> Farewell, thou art too dear for my possessing,
> And like enough thou know'st thy estimate [value].
>
> (1-2)

With quiet resignation he admits that his claims on the youth have expired. "For how do I hold thee but by thy granting?" he asks, adding that the great gift of close friendship had been granted by some mistake which must now be corrected:

> Thus have I had thee as a dream doth flatter,
> In sleep a king, but waking no such matter.
>
> (13-14)

In the next sonnet, the Poet generously states that when the youth is disposed to value him slightly he will not protest but will fight against himself and for the youth, since he is aware of his own limitations:

> Such is my love, to thee I so belong,
> That for thy right myself will bear all wrong.
>
> (13-14)

In Sonnet 89, he again speaks in behalf of the friend he is about to lose:

> Thou canst not, love, disgrace me half so ill,
> To set a form upon desirèd change,
> As I'll myself disgrace, knowing thy will.
>
> (5-7)

"Then hate me when thou wilt," he exclaims in Sonnet 90, and the youth must not delay in breaking the relationship; such delay would only prolong the Poet's suffering:

> But in the onset come; so shall I taste
> At first the very worst of fortune's might. . . .
>
> (11-12)

In the next sonnet the Poet measures the value he places upon the young man's friendship:

> Thy love is better than high birth to me,
> Richer than wealth, prouder than garments' cost. . . .
>
> (9-10)

And he understandably concedes that, with the loss of such love, he can expect only wretchedness. In the last two sonnets in the group, the Poet finds some solace in the thought that, although he is to be separated from the young man, he has no reason to believe that the youth has been unfaithful to him. The separation, it would seem, will result from the force of circumstances.

DARK BEAUTY: THE ANTI-PETRARCHAN THEME

In the discussion of the Dark Lady, it has been pointed out that Shakespeare departed radically from the strict Petrarchan tradition, according to which the lady was invariably of fair complexion. In Sonnet 127 he insists that black is now "beauty's successive [legitimate] heir" and that blond has become illegitimate, since "every tongue says beauty" should be black. Sonnet 130, which has been quoted and discussed above, carries forward this anti-Petrarchan theme amusingly. It will be recalled that the Poet practically boasts that "black wires," not golden strands, grow on his lady's head, and that he sees no "roses damasked red and white" in her cheeks. Again in Sonnet 132 he praises the dark beauty of his lady love, concluding wittily:

> Then will I swear beauty herself is black,
> And all they foul that thy complexion lack.

LOVE TURNED TO LUST

A group of nine sonnets have as their theme "Love turned to lust," again illustrating the range of topics in the sequence. The Poet depicts himself as being sensually enslaved by the fascinating Dark Lady. The theme is introduced in Sonnet 129, early in the second large division of the poems. Lust, he writes, is "Enjoyed no sooner but despised straight":

> Past reason hunted, and no sooner had,
> Past reason hated as a swallowed bait
> On purpose laid to make the taker mad. . . .
>
> (6-8)

"All this the world well knows," concludes the Poet. "Yet none knows well,/ To shun the heaven [sensation] that leads men to hell." The "Will" sonnets—135, 136, 143—place the same emphasis on the torments of lust, the term *will* meaning carnal desire. And also in Sonnet 138, with its erotic pun on the verb *lies,* the Poet speaks of the lady's "false-speaking tongue" and, making use of an erotic pun, goes on to say:

> Therefore I lie with her, and she with me
> And in our faults by lies we flattered be.
>
> (13-14)

It is of a "sensual feast" that he speaks in Sonnet 141, and in Sonnet 142 he frankly admits that such love is his sin. He accuses the lady of being promiscuous and robbing "other's beds' revenue of their rents," i.e., robbing wives of what their husbands owed them. Next, in Sonnet 144, he describes the lady as his "worser spirit" in contrast to the Fair Young Man, his "better angel," whom she seeks to corrupt. Finally, he describes his love as a fever, and states that he errs in not following the advice of Reason, his physician. "Past cure am I," he admits, in Sonnet 147, adding that "Desire is death" and that he has become "frantic-mad."

RELIGION

A religious theme is, perhaps, the last one to look for in an Elizabethan sonnet sequence, wherein love is the chief subject. But in Sonnet 146 Shakespeare developed that theme with unusual intensity. This is the one strictly religious poem in the group. In the words of Mr. Edward Hubler (*op. cit.,* p. 62), "Shakespeare presents Christianity without apology." He speaks vehemently of the inherent willfulness of the flesh and insists that only when sin is defeated will death be conquered. And sin will go down to defeat only when man has learned to emphasize the spiritual as opposed to the physical, to concern himself with his soul, the center of his "sinful earth."

> So shalt thou feed on Death, that feeds on men,
> And Death once dead, there's no more dying then.

The thought in this final couplet makes one recall the words of St.

Paul: "O death, where is thy sting? O grave, where is thy victory? The sting of death is sin..."—words hailing the triumph of the spirit.

OTHER FACETS OF INTEREST

NATURE IMAGERY

One of the many interesting elements in Shakespeare's sonnets is the nature imagery. To quote Mr. Edward Hubler once more (p. 30):

> He saw nature precisely and was always able to find the right words for her loveliness....It is to the exercise of this talent that the absence sonnets of widest fame owe their renown. Two of them ("How like a winter" and "From you I have been absent") are remembered for passages of unobtrusive melody and lines of easy grace.

Particularly, Shakespeare always wrote well on nature's morning loveliness and her plenitude. References to the beauty of early morning are many:

Sonnet 7

Lo, in the orient when the gracious light
Lifts up his burning head. . . .

(1-2)

Sonnet 29

Like to the lark at break of day arising
From sullen earth. . . .

(11-12)

Sonnet 33

Full many a glorious morning have I seen
Flatter the mountain tops with sovereign eye,
Kissing with golden face the meadows green,
Gilding pale streams with heavenly alchemy. . . .

(1-4)

Nor does the Poet neglect "swart-complexioned night" (Sonnet 28).

The seasons, to be sure, receive full attention—especially spring. Although he admits that "Rough winds do shake the darling buds of May" (18), he notes more often "April's first-born flowers" and writes with enthusiasm of "proud-pied April, dressed in all his trim" and of the "lily's white" and the "deep vermilion of the rose"(98). Elsewhere he notices "summer's green, all girded up in sheaves" (12), and he speaks of "sweet-seasoned showers" (75). Fall and winter also receive attention. With reference to fall, best known are the following opening lines from Sonnet 73:

That time of year thou mayst in me behold
When yellow leaves, or none, or few, do hang
Upon those boughs which shake against the cold,
Bare ruined choirs where late the sweet birds sang.

But fall is not always a season of sadness; it can be "teeming autumn, big with rich increase" (97). The Poet recalls the "stormy gusts of winter's day" (13) and "old December's bareness everywhere"(97). One cannot help being impressed with this seemingly effortless poetry of nature.

ASTROLOGY

Inherited from the medieval period was the idea that fate was often due to the influences of heavenly bodies, which in their eternal movements in the sky turned up good or bad fortune for mankind. Since the moon was nearest to the earth, it was deemed to have the strongest influences working for mundane variability and mutability, and particularly at times of eclipse showing its powers most obviously in such matters of essential mortality as generation and corruption. The prime importance of the moon in relation to earthly events was recognized by the Middle Ages in countless treatises on astrology and in constant application of astrological doctrine to daily life. The moon was, then, the ruling queen of variability, not only for professional astrologers, but for the unlearned and the practical man of affairs. Available was the *lunarium,* a sort of almanac listing under all the days of the month the chances, lucky or unlucky, which the moon conferred upon common undertakings. Comparable guide books relating to the influence of the stars were available. Such books continued to be popular throughout the sixteenth century. Astrological language, therefore, is common in Shakespeare and in all Elizabethan writings.

"The fault which lies in the stars," which had become an obsession in the later classical world as well as in the Middle Ages, no less interested Shakespeare and his generation. The stars, it was believed, could work for good or ill. The seven chief ones were dominating and often terrifying forces operating upon mankind. It was a brave man indeed who, like Romeo, dared to defy the stars.

In view of all this, it is not surprising that astrology (sometimes called astronomy) should find a place in Shakespeare's poems. In Sonnet 14 the first reference occurs. The Poet denies that he depends upon the stars to determine his fate:

> Not from the stars do I my judgment pluck,
> And yet me thinks I have astronomy;
> But not to tell of good or evil luck,
> Of plagues, of dearths, or seasons quality. . . .
>
> (1-4)

What he is leading up to is a familiar conceit: the Fair Young Man's beautiful eyes are the stars that guide him. In Sonnet 25 Shakespeare refers to "those who are in favor with their stars," implying that he is not numbered among them—or would not be, were it not for his love for the youth. And in Sonnet 26, he speaks of "whatever star that guides" him. Later, in Sonnet 60, he makes the first mention of "crooked eclipses" which fight against his glory. Finally, in Sonnet 107 he states that "The mortal moon hath her eclipse endured..." This line has been variously interpreted. It has been argued that Shakespeare may refer to 1588, when the Spanish Armada, thought to have assumed a crescent formation, was destroyed; to 1595, when the moon actually underwent a total eclipse; to the same year, when Queen Elizabeth I survived a critical period in her horoscope; or to 1599, when the Queen survived a dangerous illness.

THE ACTING PROFESSION

In two of the sonnets Shakespeare makes reference to the acting profession in a most interesting way. It will be recalled that he was not only a poet-dramatist but also an actor in the Lord Chamberlain's Men, which became the King's Men when James I came to the throne in 1603. There is evidence that he acted the role of the

Ghost in *Hamlet* and, in all probability, that of Prospero in *The Tempest*. He was also listed among the Dramatis Personae for Ben Jonson's *Everyman in His Humour,* which was performed at the Curtain Theatre in 1598 and was, indeed, the theatrical success of that year. There is little reason to doubt that Shakespeare played many other roles. It is inevitable, then, that reference to the acting profession should find a place in the sequence.

The first occurs in Sonnet 23, wherein the Poet compares himself to "an imperfect actor on the stage,/Who with his fear is put beside himself." Most interesting, however, is Sonnet 110. In a mood of despair, Shakespeare writes:

> Alas, 'tis true I have gone here and there
> And made myself a motley to the view. . . .
>
> (1-2)

Motley, of course, was a garment of various colors formerly worn by court jesters. It also meant a jester or a fool. It is not to be assumed that Shakespeare played the role of a clown or a fool at the Globe or elsewhere, as, for example, when his company toured the provinces. Rather, he seems to be referring to the low social status accorded actors at that time. They were officially classified with "sturdy rogues and beggars." It was for this reason that actors became the so-called "servants" of some noble or even of the Crown. Under such an arrangement they were protected from harassment by the law.

STYLE

As has been made clear, most of the sixteenth century writers of love poetry vied with each other in the use of fanciful, far-fetched metaphors and extravagant terms of praise in describing the lady who was the supposed object of their affections. Sir Philip Sidney, the most distinguished formal critic of the Elizabethan age, objected strenuously to this practice, setting forth his views in *The Defense of Poetry* (1595). Ironically, he was, on occasion, an offender himself in his sonnet sequence, *Astrophel and Stella.* In the critical work he had the following to say:

> But truly many of such writings as come under the banner
> of irresistible love; if I were a mistress, would never per-
> suade me they were in love; so coldly they apply fiery

speeches, as men that had rather read lovers' writings, and so caught up certain swelling phrases (which hang together like a man that once told me the wind was at northwest, and by south, because he would be sure to name winds enough), then that in truth they feel those passions which easily (as I think) may be revealed by that same forcibleness or *energia* (as the Greeks call it) of the writer. But let this be sufficient though short note, that all miss the right use of the material point of poesy.

Now for the outside of it, which is words, or (as I may term it) diction, it is even well worse. So is it that Honey-flowing matron Eloquence appareled, or rather disguised, in a courtesan-like painted affection: one time with so far-fetched words that many seem monster, but seem strangers, to any poor Englishman; another time, with coursing the letter, as if they were bound to follow the method of a dictionary; another time, with figures and flowers extremely winter-starved.

Judging by his practice in his sonnet sequence, Shakespeare endorsed Sidney's views. Like him he rejected "taffeta phrases, silken terms precise, thrice-piled hyperboles." In *Love's Labour's Lost,* a feast of language in which various aberrations of language are illustrated and satirized, these are a source of good comedy: Byron, the most gifted practitioner of such extravagant, affected language, is brought to the point where he vows never again to so offend against truth and reality.

Like Sidney, in his sonnets, Shakespeare rejects all such affectation, making a plea for honesty in the expression of his passion. On occasion he modestly insists that he writes only "rude lines" which are "outstripped by every pen," for he will not employ fanciful conceits and other extravagances of expression (Sonnet 32). Thus, in Sonnet 76 he writes:

> Why is my verse so barren of new pride [adornment],
> So far from variation or quick change?
> Why with the time do I not glance aside
> To new-found methods and to compounds strange?
> Why write I still all one, ever the same,
> And keep invention in a noted weed,
> That every word doth almost tell my name,
> Showing its birth, and where they did proceed?
>
> (1-8)

And in Sonnet 83 he declares that he never saw that the Fair Young Man "did painting need." Again in Sonnet 85 he states that his Muse is "tongue-tied" and in Sonnet 103 he complains: "Alack, what poverty my Muse brings forth." It is, of course, in Sonnet 130 that he satirizes most wittily the typical conceits of Petrarchanism.

Just as he will avoid affected language and high astounding terms as he applies in the sonnets noted above, so Shakespeare will not be guilty of coursing the letter—the over-use of alliteration, a practice upon which Sidney also frowned. When he does use alliteration, he does so with complete effectiveness, creating a beautiful, haunting melody. The most notable example is found in the opening lines to Sonnet 30:

> When to the sessions of sweet silent thought
> I summon up remembrance of things past. . . .

Many more lines could be cited; but the essential point is that the Poet used alliteration judiciously.

In a century fascinated by language and seeking to bring English to a state of perfection so that it could be used as effectively as any other language, ancient or modern, some writers, Spenser chief among them, revived obsolete words and introduced many archaisms into their works in an effort to enrich the language. Shakespeare would have none of this, as is made clear in Sonnet 106: he will not use an "antique pen" to praise the beauty of the youth.

It is notable that most of Shakespeare's verses are marked by what was called "monosyllabic strength." When he does use the polysyllabic term, one usually derived from the Latin, he does so because he seeks to obtain dignity and solemnity, as in Sonnet 116 (the Latin loan words are italicized):

> Let me not to the *marriage* of true minds
> *Admit impediments:* love is not love
> Which *alters* when it *alteration* finds
> Or bends with the *remover* to *remove.*

> (1-4)

Each of these terms, ultimately from the Latin, long since had been naturalized and posed no difficulty for the reader.

Nor does Shakespeare make excessive use of compounds, a practice also frowned upon by Sidney. Indeed, his use of the compound is quite a judicious one, as may be illustrated by these lines from Sonnet 30:

Then can I grieve at grievances foregone,
And heavily from woe to woe tell o'er
The sad account of *fore-bemoaned* moan,
Which I new pay as if not paid before.

(9-12)

USE OF COLOR IN THE SONNETS

The late Miss Carolyn Spurgeon pointed out the "many lovely colour groups . . . in the sonnets." The first notable example is found in Sonnet 12: violet, sable, silver, white, green. In the entire sequence color, as an element of beauty, is used no less than forty-two times. Shakespeare is particularly effective in Sonnets 73 (yellow, sunset, fire, ashen, black) and 99 (violet, purple, lily, roses, red and white). A close study of the poems reveals the fact that there are thirteen colors employed, with the great preponderance of gold, red, and green.

SELECTED CRITICISM: GENERAL

The criticism of Shakespeare's sonnets over the years has been quite favorable in general, although there have been those who found serious limitations in them, particularly in view of the fact that so many are addressed to the Fair Young Man in terms of adoration. Following are some of the representative views.

In his *Supplemental Apology,* 1797, p. 82 f., George Chalmers established himself as the first to criticize the Shakespeare of the sonnets adversely. He found them to be obscure and tedious. He did credit Shakespeare with "many happy phrases and elegant lines," but added that these are "generally darkened by conceit and marred by affectation."

More than a century later, George Gilfillan went to the opposite extreme, lauding the Poet's works (*Poetical Works of William Shakespeare and the Earl of Surrey, 1856, p. xxvi*):

Let . . . [readers] admire the Sonnets for the exquisite beauty of their imagery, which appears in more lavish abundance than even in the dramas—for the melody of their versification, a melody unparalleled for its compass, variety, and richness . . . for the blended power and sweetness of its language.

Moving up to the present century, we find many critics express ing their appreciation of the sonnets and pointing out their particular virtues. Mr. J. W. Mackail (*Approach to Shakespeare,* 1930, pp. 118f.) insisted that the sonnets, early and late, should be read and studied as poetry for their own sake. He thus rejects the historical approach and especially is distrustful of autobiographical interpretation of the poems. He placed Shakespeare above such great sonneteers as Wordsworth and Rossetti, and he concludes: "But just as Shakespeare's dramatic work eclipses that of all his contemporaries . . . so beside Shakespeare's sonnets the whole mass of other Elizabethan sonnet-literature pales and thins."

In the same year apeared *The Age of Shakespeare,* Vol. I., wherein Thomas Seccombe and J. W. Allen write interestingly and informatively about Shakespeare, the non-dramatic poet (pp. 28-29). They find the sonnets to be among "the most splendid legacies left by Elizabethan England," but argue that they remain unequal and, to some degree, conventional. No one can dispute them when they cite Sonnets 153 and 154 as "poor examples of the thoroughly conventional style." These critics also point out that Shakespeare's addressing so many of the sonnets to a man is "itself remarkable, and widely differentiates his series from those of Daniel, Lodge, Drayton, and Spenser." They state also that Shakespeare further demonstrated his originality in the Dark Lady sonnets. Unlike the Petrarchans with whom practically all of the other Elizabethan sonneteers may be classed, he does not plead or despair or rage (except against himself on occasion). "His passion is tragic with the tragedy of youthful experience." Seccombe and Allen conclude: "Two poets—and only two—of the Elizabethan Age produced love poetry in which the true note of absolute passion is struck—Shakespeare and Donne." In comparison to Donne, who "seems sometimes to set down his impressions hot and crude, in Shakespeare the passion is always mastered by the artist."

Mr. L. C. Knights ("Shakespeare's Sonnets," *Scrutiny,* 1934, II, p. 152) finds that two interests predominate in the sequence: "One is the exploration, discrimination, and judgment of modes of being —attention consciously directed towards the kind of integration of personality that is implied by the development of technique. The second is an overwhelming concern with Time."

Thomas Marc Parrott (*William Shakespeare,* 1934, p. 193) is among those who remind us that the sonnets indeed gain by selection. "All the sonnets are [not] of great and equal value. . . . Many of them are slight things, occasional verses, too often marred by the Elizabethan fondness for strained conceits. But when the poet is strongly moved he rises to very lofty heights of thought and to such perfection of expression as is matched, if matched at all, only in the plays." Mr. Parrott points out that Shakespeare is especially moved by the theme of Beauty—"beauty revealed in the person of his friend, beauty that irresistibly evokes love, beauty warred upon by Time, love triumphing over the wreckage of Time and conferring immortality on the beautiful beloved in enduring verse." The critic concludes:

> In the great sonnets . . . we may hear the voice of the supreme master of English poetry opening his heart, revealing his profoundest thoughts and most poignant emotions in accents surer of immortality than the eternity promised to the beloved friend.

The judicious views of Mr. C. S. Lewis (*English Literature in the Sixteenth Century*, 1954, pp. 498-509) must not be ignored. He proclaims the sonnets to be not only unique in a period of the Renaissance but as the supreme love-poetry of the world. And he wisely points out the difficulty one encounters if he tries to read the sequence like a novel, for "the precise mode of love which the poet declares for the man remains obscure." He concedes that the "language is too lover-like for that of ordinary male friendship," and finds "no real parallel to such language between friends in sixteenth century literature." But Mr. Lewis denies that the sonnets seem to be "the poetry of full-blown pederasty." He cites, for example, the incessant demand that the man should marry and found a family "What man in the whole world, except a father or a potential father-in-law, cares whether any other man gets married?" he asks, and he concludes: "Thus the emotion expressed by the sonnets refuses to fit into any pigeon-holes."

Finally, we may listen to Mr. W. H. Auden and learn the view of a successful contemporary poet (Introduction to *The Sonnets* Signet Classics, 1964, p. xvii f.): "Probably more nonsense has been talked and written, more intellectual and emotional energy expended in vain, on the sonnets of Shakespeare than on any other literary work in the world." Auden finds that they have become "the best touchstone for separating the sheep from the goats"—that is, those who love and understand poetry, and those who "only value poems either as historical documents or because they express feelings or beliefs of which the reader happens to approve."

Mr. Auden goes on to point out that the Shakespearean sonnet with its seven different rhymes, "almost inevitably becomes a lyric of three symmetrical quatrains finished off with an epigrammatic couplet. As a rule Shakespeare shapes his rhetorical argument in conformity with this. . . ." Major pauses occur after the fourth, eighth, and twelfth lines as a rule, although there are occasional exceptions. "It is the concluding couplet in particular which, in the Shakespearean form, can be a snare. The poet is tempted to use it, either to make a summary of the preceding twelve lines which is unnecessary, or to draw a moral which is too glib and trite." But Mr. Auden feels that Shakespeare was wise to choose the English sonnet form: English is relatively poor in rhymes in comparison with the Italian. Moreover, with the English form, the poet can accomplish certain things which are impossible for the Petrarchan form, with its sharp division between octave and sestet. For example, in Sonnets 66 and 129, Shakespeare is able "to give twelve single-line exempla of the wretchedness of this world and the horrors of lust, with accumulative effect of great power."

CRITICISM OF INDIVIDUAL SONNETS
IMAGERY IN THE EARLY SONNETS

In the early sonnets, the main and unifying image is the wealth of love. Indeed, in Sonnets 1-17, we find Shakespeare's most sustained and explicit statement of ideal love. It is interesting to see how he draws his imagery from everyday life in the world about him. In Sonnet 1, for example, he writes of love in terms of commercial gain and merchandise. He begins: "From fairest creatures we desire *increase.* . . ." The underlined term means not only Nature's increase through generation, but also commercial gain. The word looks forward to "contracted" in line 5—another obvious trade term. The sonnet ends:

Pity the world, or else this *glutton* be,
To eat the world's due, by the grave and thee.

The youth is thus told that, instead of honoring the contract with another person and so giving the world that which he owes to it, he "mak'st waste in niggarding [hoarding]." In this way Shakespeare introduces and develops the important idea of plentitude.

The same theme is repeated in Sonnet 2, but here the Poet does not call the act of loving "increase" but "use," a word not infrequently meaning "usury" and thereby linked with "niggarding" of the previous sonnet. The term "treasure" also is used in line 6, the reference being to the youth's matchless beauty. In line 8, Shakespeare speaks of "thriftless praise"—unprofitable praise. But the term "thrift" in Shakespeare's England had various meanings: (1) careful garnering of resources; (2) profit; (3) increase, or what was derived from thriving or breeding, and so "usury." This leads the Poet to lines 9-11 beginning, "How much more praise deserved thy beauty's use." So beauty is conceived as a treasure which decays unless, through love, its natural increase is made possible.

The theme is most fully developed in Sonnet 4. One should note the use of the terms *unthrifty, legacy, bequest,* and *free.* One important sense of free in this passage is "to be generous, liberal." The implication is that Nature's generosity should be matched. Shakespeare, calling the young man a "beauteous niggard" (miser), claims that he abuses the "bounteous largesse" Nature has given him and thus is a "Profitless usurer," having "traffic with [himself]" alone. Then, asks the Poet, what acceptable audit can the young man leave? The sonnet concludes:

> Thy unused beauty must be tombed with thee.
> Which used, lives th' executor to be.

In Sonnet 6, Shakespeare picks up this final couplet, or the idea imbedded therein, and again makes clear and effective use of the image of love's usury. This sonnet is notable for the ingenious multiplying of conceits and especially for the concluding pun on a legal will:

> Be not self-willed, for thou art much too fair
> To be death's conquest and make worms thine heir.

It will be noticed that the idea of "willing love" helps to expand the definition of the contract of love, and that "willing" is used not only in the legal sense but in the sense of desiring. Again the Poet insists that, once the wealth of beauty has been recognized through love for another person, it must be used if it is to increase and not decay.

Sonnet 9 is no less interesting for its imagery. Here the concept of love is not entirely distinguished from commercial wealth. Shakespeare relates the "traffickers" in love to the world at large.

The idea once more is that, when an unthrifty person makes ill use of his inherited wealth, only those among whom he squanders it benefit:

> Look what an unthrift in the world doth spend,
> Shifts but his place, for still [always] the
>   world enjoys it. . . .

(9-10)

The paradox lies in the fact that the hoarding of love's beauty is the surest way of squandering it:

> . . . beauty's waste hath in the world an end
> But kept unus'd, the user so destroys it.

(11-12)

And in the final couplet, the Poet argues that such waste must be felt by all.

These are not the only images used in the early sonnets, to be sure. In Sonnet 8 Shakespeare derived his imagery from music. The first twelve lines elaborate a comparison between music and the Fair Young Man, who is — or should be — the very embodiment of harmony. But music, "the true concord of well tunèd sounds," scolds him because he remains single — a single note, not a chord. And here we have a two-fold meaning of the key term *note:* (1) unmarried; (2) a single note. The idea is that the youth destroys the harmony he should make as part of an ensemble. The strings of a lute, for example, struck simultaneously, produce one sound, but one that is actually made up of many sounds. In this it is like a family, which is the union of father, mother, and child. The sonnet concludes:

> Whose speechless song, being many, seeming one,
> Sings this to thee, "Thou single wilt prove none."

Most critics agree with Dowden that, in the last line, Shakespeare is making reference to the proverbial saying that one is no number. Here the Poet brings to culmination the musical image, saying that a chord, being really many blended sounds, although it seems to be only one should prove to the youth that, if he remains single, he will "prove no true music."

SONNET 30: POETRY AS SOUND

Attention has already been called to the fact that this sonnet is memorable, among other things, for the effective use of alliteration. But alliteration is just one way in which a poet may enhance the melody of his work. Rhyme, of course, is another device for so doing. A third is assonance, the identity of vowel sounds in accented syllables. Sonnet 30 is no less notable for the Poet's use of this device. Note the short *e* sounds in the first two lines: When, sessions, remembered — and so elsewhere in the poem. Still another device is the attractive vowel runs, long and short. For example, consider the long sounds in line one: sweet, silent, thought; and in line 7: weep, long, since, canceled woes. It will be noted that the nasal consonants in *long since* and *cancelled* prolong the short vowels preceding. Related to this device, and contributing to the distinctive rhythm of the lines, is the variation of accents in the normally iambic pentameter lines, a way which any good poet succeeds in avoiding sing-song monotony. In line seven, one finds an example. Here there is no obvious alternation of alternating short and long syllables. Following is the pattern: __ /__ ///__ /__ /. And so in line 6: __ /__ //__ //__ /. One can well understand why the Shakespeare of the sonnets has been held to be without rival in achieving attractive rhythm, melody, and sound.

SONNET 55: THE TEXTURE OF A POEM

Sonnet 55 might very well have been used to illustrate the poem as sound, so attractive is the phrasing; but it is especially interesting as an example of superior texture, that is, the characteristic disposition of elements. As such it is one of the deservedly famous sonnets in the sequence, what with its treatment of Time in a tone of solemn dignity. One of the very best discussions of this poem is that of Mr. Hallet Smith (*Elizabethan Poetry,* 1952, pp. 178-180). It actually reads like a sonnet prefatory to a volume of love poetry. In the first four lines, the Poet dwells upon the contrast between the brightness of physical things, specifically monuments, and the memory of the youth addressed in the poem. Brightness and color are indicated by the use of the adjective *brightness*, which at no time suggests a meretricious quality as regards a prince's memorials. But in line four the Poet expresses a kind of scorn of such monuments and of gravestones in general as a means of insuring immortality.

Once bright stones may become "unswept...besmear'd with sluttish time." As Mr. Smith explains, the adjective *sluttish* suggests the lazy, careless housemaid who does not perform her duties well. Thus the aristocratic associations of the first lines are demolished and the surviving brightness of poetry is emphasized.

No less interesting is the second quatrain in which the Poet's technical virtuosity is quite impressively illustrated. Rhythm and sound combine to provide an onomatopoetic effect appropriate to the violence and disorder of war and civil strife:

> When wasteful war shall statues overturn,
> And broils [civil strife] root out the work of
>   masonry. . . .
>
> (5-6)

In the next line, "Nor Mars his sword nor war's quick fire" rhetorically conveys the idea of speed and violence. "Mars his sword," by the way, is the older genitive form, which Shakespeare uses elsewhere. The rhythmical violence of the seventh line is completely eliminated by the simplicity and quiet of the eighth line: "The living record of your memory."

The conflict between Time and forgetfulness is emphasized in the third quatrain with its impressive epithet "all oblivious enmity." The Poet speaks of the youth as "pacing forth" as if he were entering the Court, and implies that he has become the cynosure of all eyes and will inevitably "find room/Even in the eyes of all posterity." His nobility and superiority are thus insisted upon, as well as is the power of the verse to insure him immortality.

But despite this praise, so well deserved, Sonnet 55 has one limitation. It ends in a couplet of diminished force, for the Poet has said all that he needed to say in the twelve preceding lines, which had used up his emotion, leaving no need for any repetition. For the record, it may be noted that Sonnets 19, 30, 34, 42, 60, 84, 86, 91, 92, 131, 133, 139, and 141 suffer accordingly.

SONNET 60: SHIFTING IMAGERY

This is another sonnet on the subject of Time the Destroyer which has been justly praised for its imagery and superb melody. Miss Elizabeth Holmes (*Aspects of Elizabethan Imagery*, 1929, p. 42), for example, has this to say:

52

[Here] the growth of one figure out of another to shape a
continuous body of thought can be seen in its perfection,
where the fifth line. . . .is the link between the image of the
sea in flood, and that of a growing then declining light,
since it includes suggestions of both.

It has been suggested (Anon., *Blackwood's*, 1880, CXXVIII, 164)
that Robert Browning imitates the thought in this sonnet in *The
Ring and the Book,* XI, 2348-2366, where Count Guido reflects
"that all men are like waves hastening to break on the shore of
death." He thus paid tacit tribute to Shakespeare's poetic power.

A full understanding of this poem depends upon careful explication. In line 4, Shakespeare refers to the "sequent toil" of the
waves making "toward the pebbled shore." He refers to the successive waves, one following another endlessly. Beginning with the second quatrain, the Poet changes the image from the sea to the
heavens, and "nativity," or birth, is compared to the sun crawling
up the sky, called "the main [great body] of light" to distinguish it
from the "main of waters." This has been explained (Beeching, ed.,
1904) as follows:

Life beginning at a point in time within the shining sphere
of the Heavens, whose aspect is charged with fate, crawls to
maturity only to be thwarted by their fateful powers, and
time despoils the worth of his gift.

In the third quatrain the image is changed once more. Time appears in person with his conventional dart and scythe, and also
with a spade, perhaps as a gravedigger: "And nothing stands but
for his scythe to mow." And then, as in earlier sonnets, Shakespeare
declares that his verse will conquer Time itself:

And yet to times in hope, my verse shall stand
Praising thy worth, despite his cruel hand.

SONNET 64: SHAKESPEARE'S DICTION

Sonnet 64, a poem of remarkable insight and beauty, lends itself to a useful consideration of Shakespeare's diction. It is one of
the sonnets in which is found an intense consciousness of the problem of mutability. Both the object of the poet's passion and his experience of love itself are felt to be fatally exposed to the ravages of
Time: "Time will come take my love away."

In the first line the Poet speaks of Time's *fell* hand, that is, "cruel hand." In the next line he refers to "the rich proud *cost* of outworn buried *age*." The italicized terms, respectively, meaning "splendor or pomp" of "past time." *Sometime* lofty towers" of line three means "once lofty towers." And "brass *eternal*" of line 4 is "everlasting brass." In the same line "mortal rage" signifies the "rage of mortality"—of death. *Advantage* in line 6 means "inroads." In line 8 the Poet refers to "Increasing store," which means that now one increases in abundance (store) with the other's loss; no one repairs its loss with abundance taken from the other. The "interchange of *state* in line 9 stands for "interchange of condition." But *state* as used in the next line means "greatness," which is *confounded*, or destroyed. The final line may be paraphrased as follows: "But weep because it has that which it fears to lose."

SONNET 73: STRUCTURE

This well-known sonnet especially illustrates the virtues of the English form at its best. In the first quatrain the Poet compares himself to autumn leaves; in the second, to twilight; and in the third, to dying embers. From the union of these images emerges the dominant idea of impending death. There follows the completely justifiable couplet addressed to the young man and pointing out the conclusion to be drawn from the preceding lines:

This thou perceiv'st which makes thy love more strong
To love that well which thou must leave ere long.

Note that there is a pause after each quatrain, the longest coming appropriately after the third. This was the customary usage among the writers of sonnets in the English form.

SONNET 94: VARIED INTERPRETATIONS

The end of the poem is the beginning, according to the late T. S. Eliot; that is, in the democracy of criticism varying interpretations are deemed acceptable. This point of view may be illustrated by reference to selected critical comments on Sonnet 94. According to Wyndham (ed. *Sonnets*, 1898) Shakespeare first advances the argument of those who, with an outward beauty which is the source of temptation, are themselves cold and not easily tempted. They are the owners and masters of their destiny; but, in contrast, those whose beauty not only tempts but also leads them into temptation are the dispensers of it. As a symbol of the first, the Poet takes a flower which is sweet to the world around it, although it blossoms and dies to itself, self-contained and unrewarding. As a symbol of the second, the same flower is infected with a canker, in which case it is more offensive than a weed.

Mr. William Empson (*Some Versions of Pastoral*, 1935, p. 89 ff.) has his own explanation of the poem, which he insists is "a piece of grave irony." He tells us that, according to Shakespeare, superior individuals remain aloof and never submit to temptation. Nor in so doing are they being selfish, for they unconsciously do good, like the flowers. The Youth, the Poet continues, must be, indeed already is, quite like them. Yet even such superior individuals must remain alert not to fall from perfection if they are to avoid becoming the worst, just as "Lilies that fester, smell far worse than weeds."

A third interpretation is that of Mr. Edward Hubler (*op. cit.,* pp. 102-106), who approaches the poem in the light of Shakespeare's other works and who is quite aware of the fact that the poem "has been the object of more critical analyses than any other sonnet." Mr. Hubler points out that it makes use of Shakespeare's most familiar imagery and that the basic idea of the sonnet is to be found everywhere in the poet-dramatist's works. He emphasizes the irony of the first two quatrains: "It is preposterous on the face of things to proclaim as the inheritors of heaven's graces those who are 'as stone.' It can be other than ironical only to the cynic, for even the hardhearted man thinks of himself as generous and cherishes an abstract admiration for warmth." Mr. Hubler finds the octave to be "Swiftian in both method and force," the poet stating in specious terms that which he clearly considered to be false: "those men whose appearance does not square with reality, whose deeds do not fulfill their promise, who move others while remaining cold, are proclaimed the heirs to heaven's graces." Elsewhere in his works, Shakespeare insisted that "the sense of living without regard for others is intolerable," and he cites the examples of Rosencrantz and Guilderstern, Goneril and Regan, and others. At the end of the octave ("Others but stewards of their excellence") there is a full stop, and then the Poet introduces the familiar image of the summer's flower, which is beautiful despite the fact that it lives unto itself alone: an obvious analogy. Earlier and often in the sequence he had praised the flower's beauty, but saw it only as one of its attributes and not necessarily as the most important one. The beauty, he argued, is increased by the flower's odor, which represents that which is usefully good. In Sonnet 69, for example, he writes:

> But why thy odour matcheth not thy show,
>   The soil is this, that thou does common grow.
>
> (13-14)

And in Sonnet 54:

> O, how much more doth beauty beauteous seem
> By that sweet ornament which truth doth give.
> The rose looks fair, but fairer we it deem
> For that sweet odour which doth live in it. . . .
>
> (1-4)

In Sonnet 94, the flower, isolated, does not fulfill its function, despite its beauteous form. And "if it should meet with infection" (that is, if the expression of its function should be perverted), its odor (that is, its essence, its soul, its human utility as expressed in the deeds of the young man and the perfume of the flower) becomes worse than that of weeds—worse, that is, than that form which nothing was expected.

Mr. Walter Kaufman (*From Shakespeare to Existentialism,* 1960, pp. 5-8) vehemently rejects Mr. Hubler's interpretation of Sonnet 94, which he believes "celebrates Shakespeare's un-Christian ideal, which was also the ideal of Nietzsche. . . ." With reference to the first two lines of the poem—

> They that have power to hurt and will do none,
> That do not do the thing they most do show . . .

—Mr. Kaufman finds what he calls an exellent commentary in a passage from the German philosopher's chapter "On Those Who Are Sublime" in *Thus Spake Zarathustra:*

> One who was sublime I saw today, one who was solemn, an ascetic of the spirit; oh, how my soul laughed at his ugliness! . . . As yet he has not overcome his deed. . . . As yet his torrential passion has not become still in beauty. Verily, it is not in satiety that his desire shall grow silent, be submerged, but in beauty. Gracefulness is part of the graciousness of the great-souled. . . . There is nobody from whom I want beauty as much as from you who are powerful: let

56

your kindness be your final self-conquest. Of all evil I deem you capable: therefore I want the good from you. Verily, I have often laughed at the weaklings who thought themselves good because they had no claws.

"Shakespeare, too," the critic continues, "celebrates the man who has claws but does not use them." Kaufman sees nothing preposterous or ironic, as Hubler does, in the Poet's saying that the inheritors of heaven's graces are those who are as stone. "What seems preposterous to a Christian reader need not have struck a Roman or a Spartan as unseemly." He reminds his readers that Shakespeare was an actor and admonishes those "who would rather not believe that Shakespeare, the poet, moving others, was himself as stone. . . ." He sees the Poet, then, as one who endorsed the idea of the aloof superman, one who looked with contempt upon the common man and who viewed religion as mere superstition. Shakespeare himself would surely be among those quite startled at this bit of impressionistic criticism.

SONNET 116: AN EXERCISE IN DEFINITION

The essence of love and friendship for Shakespeare, it is apparent, is reciprocity or mutuality. In Sonnet 116, for example, the ideal relationship is referred to as "the marriage of true minds," a state which can be realized by the dedicated and faithful:

> Let me not to the marriage of true minds
> Admit impediments.

(1-2)

These lines echo the marriage services in the Book of Common Prayer: "If any of you know cause or just impediment . . ." Thus we understand the Poet's attitude toward his subject. He then proceeds to define such love, first negatively—that is, explaining what it is not, always an effective rhetorical device:

> love is not love
> Which alters when it alteration finds,
> Or bends with the remover to remove.

(2-4)

He continues this formal method of definition now by advancing an affirmative definition:

> . . . it is an ever-fixèd mark,
> That looks on tempests and is never shaken;
> It is the star of every wandering bark,
> Whose worth's unknown, although his height be taken.
>
> (5-8)

The "ever-fixèd mark," to be sure, is the traditional sea mark and guide for mariners, the North Star, whose value is inestimable, although its altitude has been determined. The star, unlike physical beauty, we are told, is not subject to the ravages of Time. And so true love, which is not "Time's fool" (plaything, as here used). In his definition Shakespeare then introduces the great concepts of Space and Time, applying them to his idea of true love:

> Love alters not with his brief hours and weeks,
> But bears it out to the edge of doom.
>
> (11-12)

"Bears it out" means survives, and "edge of doom," Judgment Day. Finally, with absolute conviction, the Poet challenges others to find him wrong in his definition:

> If this be error and upon [against] me proved,
> I never writ, and no man ever loved.

This is his standard of friendship and love which he hopes that he and the Fair Young Man can achieve.

SONNET 129: THE STRINDBERGIAN MOOD

Perhaps no poem illustrates how far Shakespeare could depart from the Petrarchan tradition of love poetry than Sonnet 129, which has been called an almost Strindbergian poem on the power of lust. In a hortatory mood he writes:

> . . . lust
> Is perjur'd, murderous, blood, full of blame,
> Savage, extreme, rude, cruel, not to trust. . . .
>
> (2-4)

Here especially he asks why the heart should be moved by what he knows to be worthless. But, obviously bound by passion, he cannot escape despite his better self, and he endeavors to convince himself that the Dark Lady is better than he knows her to be. As R. C. Trench wrote (*Household Book*, 1868, p. 392), "The bitter delusion of all sinful pleasures, the reaction of a swift remorse which inevitably dogs them, Shakespeare must have most deeply felt, as he has expressed himself upon it most profoundly." As a testimonial of profound and powerful emotions, this poem, in the words of J. A. Symonds (*Sir Philip Sidney*, 1886, p. 153), is "the most completely powerful sonnet in our literature." Bernard Shaw (*Nation,* London, 1910, VIII, 543) described it as "the most merciless passage in English literature."

The poem requires little annotation. *Expense* in the first line means "expenditure"; in the same line *spirit* has the double meaning of "vital power" and "semen." *Past* in lines 6 and 7 means "beyond." And *made* in line 9 means "when experienced." *Dream*, line 12, may well refer to a nightmare in view of the context in which it is used. Finally the *heaven* referred to in the last line is the "sensation" (or possibly "place") of bliss.

QUESTIONS

1. What evidence can you adduce to support the belief that the sonnets are autobiographical?

2. Which sonnets seem to you to be most conventional and imitative?

3. In which sonnets does Shakespeare express originality?

4. What are three ways in which he departs radically from the Petrarchan tradition?

5. Select two sonnets from each of the two major divisions. How do they differ in mood and the treatment of love?

6. What are the structural virtues of Sonnet 73 as compared, for example, with Sonnet 30?

7. In which sonnets does the Poet pun wittily — and sometimes shockingly?

8. What evidence is there that Shakespeare sought to avoid af-

fected and pretentious language? To what extent do you believe he succeeded?

9. What structural virtues do you find in the Shakespearean form of the sonnet as opposed to the Italian? What are the dangers which are not always avoidable?

10. In the sonnets, what views does Shakespeare express as regards (a) the nature of true love; (b) the miseries of misplaced love; (c) the obligations of stewardship?

11. What are five adjectives used to describe time in the first large division?

12. In what ways does Shakespeare indicate that time may be conquered? In which of the ways do the poems themselves prove to be right?

13. What do you take to be the respective ages of the man addressed and the poet? Why?

14. What evidence do you find that the young man is of high social rank?

15. Aside from love, what themes does the Poet develop in the sonnets?

16 What views of the acting profession does Shakespeare advance? Why?

17. What words does the Poet use to describe (a) the man addressed; (b) the Dark Lady?

18. What lapses in the character of the youth does Shakespeare note? What is his reaction thereto?

19. Sonnet 146 has been described as one of the two most powerful poems in the sequence. What do you find to be the source of its power?

20. What use does Shakespeare make of nature in the sonnets?

BIBLIOGRAPHY

Bray, Sir Denys de Saumarez. *The Original Order of Shakespeare's Sonnets.* London, 1925.

_____. *Shakespeare's Sonnet Sequence.* London, 1938.

Chambers, Sir E. K. *Shakespearean Gleanings.* London, 1944.

Cuttwell, Patrick. *The Shakespearean Moment,* New York, 1960.

Herrnstein, Barbara, ed. *Discussions of Shakespeare's Sonnets.* New York, 1964.

Hubler, Edward. *The Sense of Shakespeare's Sonnets.* Princeton 1952.

_____, Northrop Frye, Leslie A. Fiedler, Stephen Spender, and R. P. Blackmuir. *The Riddle of Shakespeare's Sonnets.* New York, 1962.

Knights, L. C. *Some Shakespearean Themes.* London, 1960.

Krieger, Murray. *A Window to Criticism: Shakespeare's Sonnets and Modern Poetics.* Princeton, 1964.

Landry, Hilton. *Interpretations of Shakespeare's Sonnets.* Princeton 1964.

Leishman, J. B. *Themes and Variations in Shakespeare's Sonnets* London, 1961.

Lever, J. W. *The Elizabethan Love Sonnet.* London, 1956.

Prince, F. T. *The Sonnet from Wyatt to Shakespeare.* Stratford-on Avon Studies, 2, 1960.

Quennell, Peter. *Shakespeare.* New York, 1963.

Robertson, J. M. *The Problems of Shakespeare's Sonnets.* London 1926.

Rollins, Hyder E., ed. *A New Variorum Edition of Shakespeare: the Sonnets.* 2 vols. London, 1944.

Rouse, A. L. *Shakespeare's Sonnets.* New York, 1964.

Willen, Gerald and Victor B. Reed. *A Casebook on Shakespeare's Sonnets.* New York, 1964.

Wilson, J. Dover. *An Introduction to the Sonnets of Shakespeare.* New York, 1964.

NOTES